Text copyright © 2023 by Matthew Oliphant
Artwork copyright © 2023 by Kristin Valentine

All rights reserved. No part of this publication may be reproduced, stored or transmitted in any form or by any means, electronic, mechanical, photocopying, recording, scanning, or otherwise without written permission from the publisher unless for purposes of critique or review. It is illegal to copy this book, post it to a website, or distribute it by any other means without permission. The copyright for this book expires December 31, 2048. After this date the authors consider it to be in the Public Domain. Because 70 years is too long.

This book is entirely a work of fiction. The names, characters and incidents portrayed in it are the work of the author's imagination. Any resemblance to actual persons, living or dead, events or localities is entirely coincidental. The dogs, on the other hand, are real and their likenesses are used with permission from their person. Do us a favor: take good care of yourself today.

First edition October 2023

ISBN 979-8-9868545-7-1 (paperback, premium color)
ISBN 979-8-9868545-9-5 (paperback, standard color)
Library of Congress Control Number: 2023918460

matthewoliphant.com/ilyd

I LOVE YOUR DOG!

How to Yell at Strangers in a Socially Acceptable Way

A picture book for grownups who forgot how to be silly in public.

First, this book should be read out loud—even if you're the only one in the room, but especially if there are other people. Read it in a cafe, at school or work, or, better yet, on the bus.

Please remember to raise your voice and project when you read the phrase, **I LOVE YOUR DOG**. Like, right now you should have said that really loud. If we've learned anything from the Internet, allcaps means yelling.

Second, this is actually a manifesto—but not the kind that can get you thrown into jail, ideally, for our sake. The main premise of the manifesto is: Dogs are great and reminding each other of that fact on a daily basis spreads cheeriness. And cheeriness is needed.

Especially after ... *waves hand* ... everything.

This book doesn't cover all aspects of life with dogs, but we would like to take the opportunity, while we have your attention, to note that you really need to pick up the poop. That's not the dog's responsibility, it's yours. Just effing do it.

Sincerely,

Matthew & Kristin

when?

When should you yell, "I LOVE YOUR DOG"?

Just now when you read that sentence. We put it in allcaps for a reason.

When you are walking by a dog, and their person, and will continue to your destination without stopping. Adding a squeal of delight is acceptable.

When you are driving somewhere and can *safely* yell it out the window without crashing into anything or, and we can't stress this enough, anyone.

Don't yell it:

When there are no dogs around. Well, YMMV.

When your motivation is to get the dog's person to notice you. See page 25 about not making it awkward.

When it's actually a cat.

Let's start with something easy.

A simple flow chart to help you decide
when to yell **I LOVE YOUR DOG**.

is it a dog?

practice

Pepper

→ no.
best not.

Sadie

→ yes!
YELL IT NOW!

Ever had to call customer support and when you finally got a person on the line—whose job it is to answer the phone and listen—and you tell them your issue ... and for some reason they ask you to repeat yourself because they weren't ready to listen?

That's why we start a well-landed **I LOVE YOUR DOG** with a simple, "Hi."

Missy

stick the landing

Should you yell anything other than, "I LOVE YOUR DOG"?

Eh ... you can, but your **I LOVE YOUR DOG** may not land as well as you want. Lead off with a **Hey, Hi, Hello, or Yo**—something short to get the dog's person's brain ready to notice that someone is talking to them.

Do not use:

Excuse me... *(as you are not selling something or asking for spare change)*

or

Hey, [insert mean word]... *(don't be mean)*

or the rather non-sequitur

My, what wonderful weather we are having today I LOVE YOUR DOG!

even though it is quite enjoyable to non-sequit

Which dogs should be yelled about?

Not enough people are discussing this important topic.

You might be surprised (or might not, we don't know you) to hear that all dogs are the bestest dogs.

All of them.

Even dogs who are aggressive because we all know, or will know at the end of this sentence, that "bad dog" really means "the dog's person didn't train the dog."

That said, here are some dogs that are the bestest: My dog, your dog, that dog you saw while jogging the other day, the dog who is barking while you're in a meeting, tiny dogs, big dogs, and even dogs who like carrots.

See *Exhibit A* for reference.

Stuart

exhibit a

Feeling Names™*

There will come a time, when you've had a lot of **I LOVE YOUR DOG** practice, where you look at a dog, who is not your own, and think, "That dog's name is definitely Foofers." You are not incorrect to think this.

It is perfectly acceptable, nay, admirable, to give dogs very silly, yet appropriate Feeling Names. It's the name that springs to mind when you see the dog and it feels just right.

You might meet a dog named Milo.

Milo is a great name, but you know, in your heart of hearts, that Milo is really called *Sir Schnoofsalot*.

Milo

*not actually trademarked. we thought it looked cool with the ™.

Bork-Bork

Borfmortle

Sniffledypippldy

Forfles

Mop-Mop

Pibbly

Floofee

Reginald von Barkington III

Snoozypoops

16

now what?

Can you interact with a dog you just yelled about?

Yes, if:

It's your dog.
You're invited by the dog's person. *See next page*.
There is no third option.

No, but:

You *can* go about your day imaging it.

Bacchus

"Thanks, you can pet ＿＿＿!"

ohno.

You yelled **I LOVE YOUR DOG** and the dog's person said you can pet the dog! Now what?!

Remain calm. Outwardly.

Inwardly, now is the time to squee. **SQUEE!** Make sure the dog also gives approval for this petting, then get to it. Scritch their neck, rub their chin, pat their bum. Stay away from the tail.

If ... and *BIG IF* here ... bellyrubs come into play, it is entirely appropriate to outwardly squee. **SQUEE!**

Thank the dog (one final scritch), thank the dog's human. Go back to what you were doing. Your day just got better—and so did theirs.

What's the best way to compliment a dog?

There is no wrong way.

If you can't think of anything, try:

Cutie puppy!

Sweetie baby!

Your ears are so big!

I am experiencing acute Cute Aggression! It's a real thing! I have a doctor's note!

[internal squeeing intensifies]*

MOCHA

*yes, say this out loud.

What's the best way to compliment a dog's human?

Uh ... that's not what this book is about.

There's no need to compliment the dog's person.

But, this needs to be said ... *because people*.

Not you, you're great! Probably. We mean other people, who are not you, who didn't buy this book...

When you yell **I LOVE YOUR DOG** (like you should have just now) keep in mind it's a joy-driven compliment, not a battlecry or a catcall (literally and figuratively).

Harold

whisper yell because she's meditating with the moon

whisper-yell it now!

Let's not make this awkward.

Remember a few pages ago we said to not yell it when your motivation is to get the dog's person to notice you?

You are meant to yell (or loud-whisper) **I LOVE YOUR DOG** then immediately go back to what you were doing before you yelled **I LOVE YOUR DOG**.

You're yelling **I LOVE YOUR DOG** and spreading cheer because it is good and right to do so.

You're **not** making it about you. When you continue on with your day, you're communicating that you're not trying to interrupt the dog's person's day—you're only sharing your excitement about their dog.

Continuing on with your day gives the person an out and that's a kind thing to do.*

*Especially for the 49.584% of the planet's population who's SUPER TIRED of being yelled at by strangers.

What if someone yells it at you?

Stay calm.

Look to see if you have a dog.

If you do, reply "thank you" with the same tone and volume with which you received the **I LOVE YOUR DOG**.

Pro-Tip

You don't even have to look at the person who yelled **I LOVE YOUR DOG**. Ideally, you should look at your dog while replying.

If you don't have a dog ... maybe back away slowly and definitely don't make eye contact.

Arthur

Tink

hey, waitaminute...

What's all this yelling actually about?

To be honest, the purpose of this book wasn't to teach you how to yell at strangers in a socially acceptable way, as our snappy subtitle suggests.

That was a ruse!

We want to get more people in the world—you and also the person next to you if you're reading this with someone—helping to spread cheeriness by yelling **I LOVE YOUR DOG** in public.

mwahahaha!

Make no mistake: this is not world-changing stuff. But, it might actually be day-changing for someone and their little dog, too.

Thank you for letting us trick you into cheering other people up!

One last time to practice before you go out into the world to spread cheer.

thank you

Brandy

Ana–Marlo & James
Arthur–Natalie
Bacchus & Brandy–Kristin
Bailey, Baxter, & Brewtis–Angela
Cole & Milo–Sara
Hamish–Beth

Missy & Mocha–Danielle
Peanut & Sadie–Jennifer
Pebble–Sagan
Ruby–Moira
Stuart–Samantha
Tink–Laura

about / dedication

When not talking about himself in third-person, Matthew has returned to writing after a 20 year break. He lives with his family in Portland, Oregon and is working on another book just for you. Who knows where he is now or of what he is yet to dream.

Kristin was quite happy paint dogs (and a cat!) for this project—the paintings are acrylic gouache on watercolor paper. She lives in Bellingham, Washington where she bikes, makes pots, and always enjoys being outside with her pup.

Matthew

Dear, Sagan. Without you, and your persistant, "Can we please get a dog," when you were 10, we would not have a dog. I don't like dogs. Well ... I didn't before Pebble.

It took me almost 10 years to go from being afraid of dogs to yelling **I LOVE YOUR DOG** at people. All thanks to you.

Kristin

Thank you, Matthew. It is always a pleasure to work on projects together—especially when dogs are involved.

To Brandy, who was a great lover of ear scratches, absolutely cared nothing for rules about beds or furniture, and was truly the most gentle creature on the planet. You are missed.

www.ingramcontent.com/pod-product-compliance
Lightning Source LLC
Chambersburg PA
CBHW041927080125
20078CB00035B/249